Janice VanCleave's

Play and Find Out

about

Nature

Easy Experiments for Young Children

John Wiley & Sons, Inc.

New York • Chichester • Weinheim • Brisbane • Singapore • Toronto

S

This text is printed on acid-free paper.

Published by John Wiley & Sons, Inc.
All rights reserved. Published simultaneously in Canada.

The publisher and author have made every reasonable effort to ensure that the experiments and activities in the book are safe when conducted as instructed but assume no
responsibility for any damage caused or sustained while performing the experiments or
activities in this book. Parents, guardians, and/or teachers should supervise young readers
who undertake the experiments and activities in this book.

Library of Congress Cataloging-in-Publication Data

VanCleave, Janice Pratt.
    [Play and find out about nature}
    Janice VanCleave's play and find out about nature : 50 fun, easy experiments and
ideas for young children.
       p.   cm.   — (Janice VanCleave's play and find out series)
    Includes index.
    Summary: Provides instructions for fifty nature experiments and activities involving
both plants and animals.
    ISBN 0-471-12939-9 (cloth : alk. paper).—ISBN 0-471-12940-2 (pbk. : alk. paper)
    1. Biology—Experiments—Juvenile literature. 2. Nature—Experiments—Juvenile
literature. 3. Nature study—Experiments—Juvenile literature. [1. Biology—Experiments.
2. Nature—Experiments. 3. Nature study—Experiments. 4. Experiments.] I. Title.
II. Series: VanCleave, Janice Pratt. Play and find out series.
QH3116.5.V366   1997
574—dc20

96-2865

Printed in the United States of America
10 9 8 7 6 5 4 3 2 1

Dedication

This book is dedicated to a special lady who is ever on the lookout for ways to make learning fun and exciting for her special students—her own children. She field-tested this book with them and shared it with other parents listed below. Not only has she been my courier in delivering materials, she has also given me invaluable clues on how to catch the interest of young children. What fun I have had listening to the exciting experiences she and her children shared as they learned and played together while reviewing this book! But the most important part has been my exchange of ideas with my friend, Anne Skrabanek.

Acknowledgments

I would like to thank the parents and children of a Waco, Texas, Homeschool-Co-Op for assisting me in testing the experiments in this book. They are Greg, Mona, Bethany, and Michael Bond; Ken, Carol, Matthew, Emily, and Sarah Keil; Kent, Debbie, Anna, Kent Jr., Steven, and Andrew Mathias; Ron, Anne, Sarah, Benjamin, and Rebecca Skrabanek; and John, Diana, Joseph, Abigail, and Samuel Warren.

A special note of appreciation to another friend, Laura Fields Roberts. Laura not only field-tested the experiments in this book, but she shared with me the fun she and her students had via photographs and letters. These are the students from St. Matthews Elementary School in Louisville, Kentucky who under the direction of Laura and her coworker, Sandra Williams Petrey, played and found out about nature: Tricia Baldwin, Brittany Ballinger, Amanda Boden, Antonio Brown, Stephanie Coy, Courtney Duffey, Alexandra Foote, Jessica Gilbert, Kaitlin Goodhew, Chelsey Hallett, Jessica Hamilton, Dane Hardy, Taylor Hawkins, Emily Jimmerson, William Long, Amy Love, Saphire Miller, Taylor Mouser, David Presnell, Hannah Rapp, Kristin Shattuck, Beth Spurr, Sarah Thomas, and Orenzio Tobin.

Again, let me say thanks to Laura for using the experiments in this book to design a program for a 1995 Future Minds Summer Enrichment Class (a nonprofit organization). The pre-kindergarten students in the class were Ryan Garvey, Ethan Grunst, David Knox, Jordan Kruger, Rebecca Saag, G. Aaron Tallent, Ashleigh Salomon-Vetter, Zachary Wall, Max Yanker, and Dylan Yussman.

Contents

A Letter from Janice VanCleave

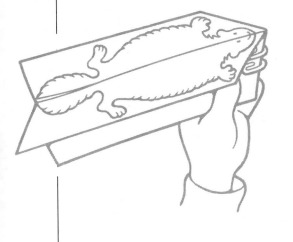

Dear Friends,

Welcome to science playtime!

The scientific play activities in this book are about plants and animals. Young children generally love animals and plants, and they are excited to learn about them. Actual animals aren't used in any of the experiments, but expect your child to be delighted by models of such things as flying squirrels and bird beaks that can catch popcorn.

Discovering things on their own gives kids a wonderful feeling of success. All they need is your friendly guidance, a few good ideas, and their natural curiosity. This book is full of fun ideas. It contains instructions for more than 50 simple, hands-on experiments inspired by questions from real kids. While you play together, your child will find out the answers to questions such as "Why does a dog pant?" "What's inside a seed?" and lots of other things that children wonder about.

So get ready to enter into a science adventure.

Playfully yours,

Janice VanCleave

Before You Begin

 Read the experiment completely before starting. When possible, practice the experiment by yourself prior to your science playtime. This increases your understanding of the topic and makes you more familiar with the procedure and the materials. If you know the experiment well, it will be easier for you to give your child instructions and answer questions.

Select a place to work. The kitchen table is usually the best place for the activities. It provides space and access to an often needed water supply.

Choose a time. There is no best time to play with your child, and play should be the main point when doing the experiments in this book. Select a time when you will have the fewest distractions so that you can complete the activity. If your family has a schedule, you may allot a specific amount of time for the activity. You may want to set an exact starting time so that the child can watch the clock and become more familiar with time. Try to schedule 5 to 10 minutes at the close of each session to have everyone clean up.

Collect supplies. You will have less frustration and more fun if all the materials are ready before you start. (See "Tips on Materials" in the box on the next page.)

⑤ ***Do not rush through the experiment.*** Follow each step carefully, and for sure and safe results, never skip steps or add your own. Safety is of the utmost importance, and it is good science technique to teach children to follow instructions when doing a science experiment.

Tips on Materials

- Some experiments call for water. If you want everything to be at the worktable, you can supply water in a pitcher or soda bottle.

- Extra paper towels are always handy for accidental spills, especially if the experiment calls for liquids. A large bowl can be used for waste liquids, and the bowl can be emptied in the sink later.

- To save time, you can precut some of the materials (except string; see below).

- Do not cut string in advance, because it generally gets tangled and is difficult to separate. You and the child can measure and cut the string together.

- You may want to keep labeled shoe boxes filled with basic supplies that are used in many experiments, such as scissors, tape, marking pens, and so forth.

- The specific sizes and types of containers listed in the material lists are those used when these experiments were tested. This doesn't mean that substituting a different type of container will result in an experimental failure. Substitution of supplies should be a value judgment made after you read an experiment to determine the use of the supplies. For example, you could replace a 12-ounce (360-ml) paper cup to plant beans with a plastic container that is equal, or nearly equal, to 12 ounces (360 ml).

- For large groups, multiply the supplies by the number in the group so that each person can perform the experiment individually. Some of the supplies (glue, for instance) can be shared, so read the procedure to determine this ahead of time.

⑥ ***Have fun!*** Don't worry if the child isn't "getting" the science principle, or if the results aren't exactly perfect. If you feel the results are too different from those described, reread the instructions and start over from step 1.

⑦ ***Enjoy the wonder of participating in the learning process.*** Remember, it is OK for your child not to discover the scientific explanation. For example, when you perform the experiment "Glider," the child may be too excited to stop sailing the paper squirrel and listen to your explanation of how some squirrels "fly." Don't force the child to listen. Join in the fun and make a magic moment to remember. Later, when questions arise about animals that fly, you can remind the child of the fun time that you had doing the "Glider" experiment, then repeat the experiment, providing the explanation.

Basic Life-Forms

Building Blocks

Round Up These Things

cooking pot
6-ounce (170-g) package of
  lemon gelatin dessert mix
1-cup (250-ml) measuring cup
1-quart (1-liter) resealable
  plastic bag
2-quart (2-liter) bowl
small plum or other fruit of
  comparable size
5 to 6 peanuts (with or without their shells)

Later You'll Need

round toothpicks
modeling clay

1 **ADULT STEP** Using the cooking pot and gelatin dessert mix, prepare the mix according to the instructions on the box. Allow the gelatin to cool to room temperature.

2 Use the measuring cup to scoop the cooled gelatin into the resealable bag. Seal the bag and place it in the bowl.

3 Set the bowl with the bag in the refrigerator to chill until the gelatin is firm (about 3 to 4 hours).

4 Remove the bowl from the refrigerator.

5 Using your finger, insert a plum into the center of the gelatin.

6 Use your finger to insert the peanuts in the gelatin.

7 Seal the bag.

8 Hold the bag over the bowl as you gently squeeze the bag. (The bowl is used in case you squeeze too hard and the bag opens.) Observe the shape of the bag. Set the bag on a table and observe the shape of the bag. Then, pick it up and look at the shape again.

9 Put the bag in the refrigerator until it is needed for the experiment "Stiff."

So Now We Know

Cells are the building blocks of all living things. The bag of gelatin represents a model of an animal cell. It has a thin, flexible lining which holds the cell parts (the bag), the jellylike fluid that the cell parts float in (the gelatin), the control center (the plum), and the power stations where food is changed into energy (the peanuts). Like the cell model, animal cells are soft and get squeezed out of shape when something pushes against them. This change is not permanent, as you observed when you placed the bag on the table. A cat is soft because of its soft cells, but its fur also makes it feel soft.

More Fun Things to Know and Do

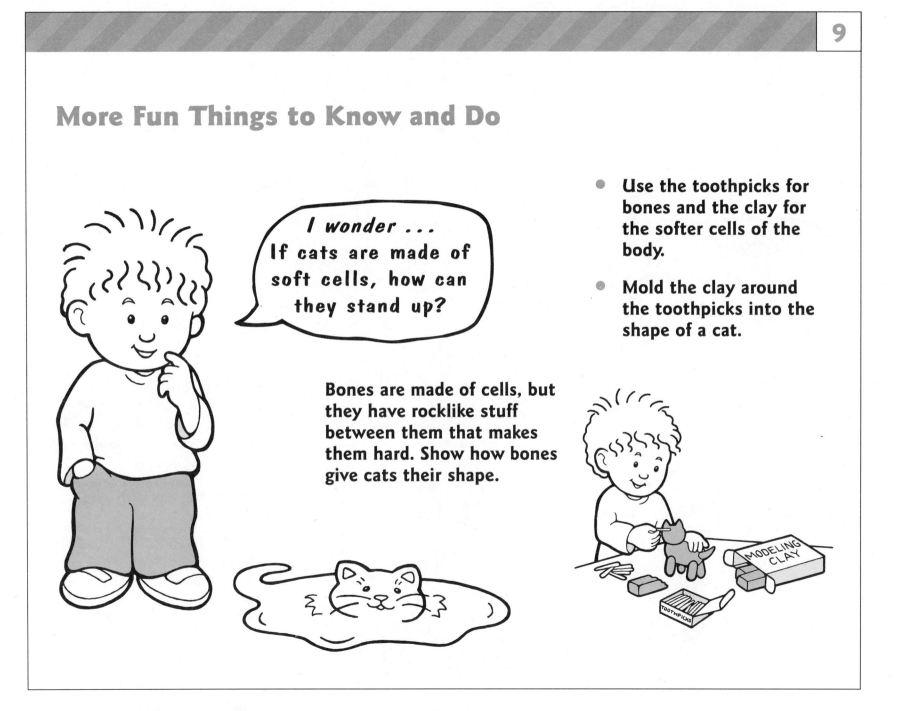

I wonder . . .
If cats are made of soft cells, how can they stand up?

Bones are made of cells, but they have rocklike stuff between them that makes them hard. Show how bones give cats their shape.

- Use the toothpicks for bones and the clay for the softer cells of the body.

- Mold the clay around the toothpicks into the shape of a cat.

Stiff

I wonder ... Do plants have bones?

Let's find out!

Round Up These Things

bag of gelatin and bowl from "Building Blocks"
4 to 6 green grapes
small shoe box with a lid

Later You'll Need

2 small bowls
tap water
knife (to be used only by an adult)
cutting board
cucumber

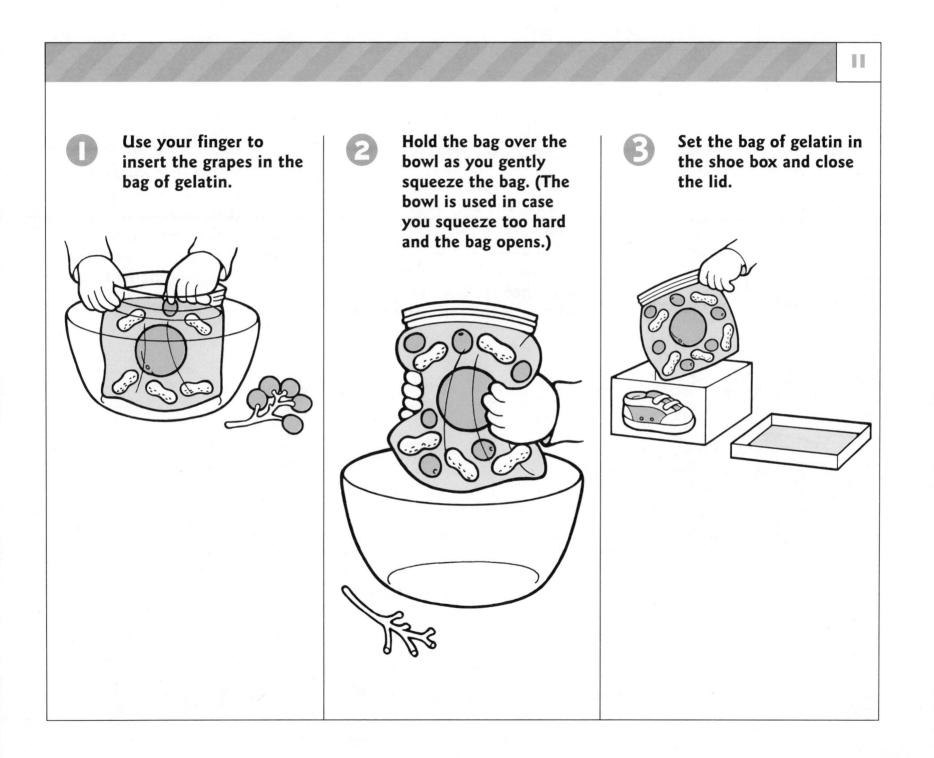

① Use your finger to insert the grapes in the bag of gelatin.

② Hold the bag over the bowl as you gently squeeze the bag. (The bowl is used in case you squeeze too hard and the bag opens.)

③ Set the bag of gelatin in the shoe box and close the lid.

4 Hold the shoe box and gently squeeze it.

So Now We Know

Plants, like animals, are made of cells. The bag of gelatin and the shoe box represent a model of a plant cell. Plants and animals have some cell parts that are the same. But two plant cell parts that animals don't have are green food factories (the grapes) and a stiff covering around the cell (the shoe box). Plants do not have bones to give them shape. Instead, the firm cell covering helps to do this.

More Fun Things to Know and Do

Water inside plant cells also makes a plant firm. Vegetables that are kept in a container of water stay crisp because water fills the cells. Show this by testing cucumber slices in and out of water.

- Fill one of the bowls half full with water.

- ADULT STEP Use the knife and cutting board to slice the cucumber.

- Place half the cucumber slices in each bowl.

- Allow the bowls to stand undisturbed for one day.

- Remove the cucumber slices from each bowl and break each in half by bending it with your hands. Determine which cucumbers are firmer, the ones that were in water or the ones that were not.

Water Critters

I wonder ...
Are there critters
you can't see in
pond water?

Let's find
out!

Round Up These Things

2 left shoes: 1 large,
  1 small
3 sheets of construc-
  tion paper: 1 white,
  1 red, 1 blue
pencil
scissors
glue
glitter (any color)
marking pen

Later You'll Need

scissors
3 sheets of construction
  paper: 1 yellow, 1 green,
  1 blue
glue
glitter
string
marking pen

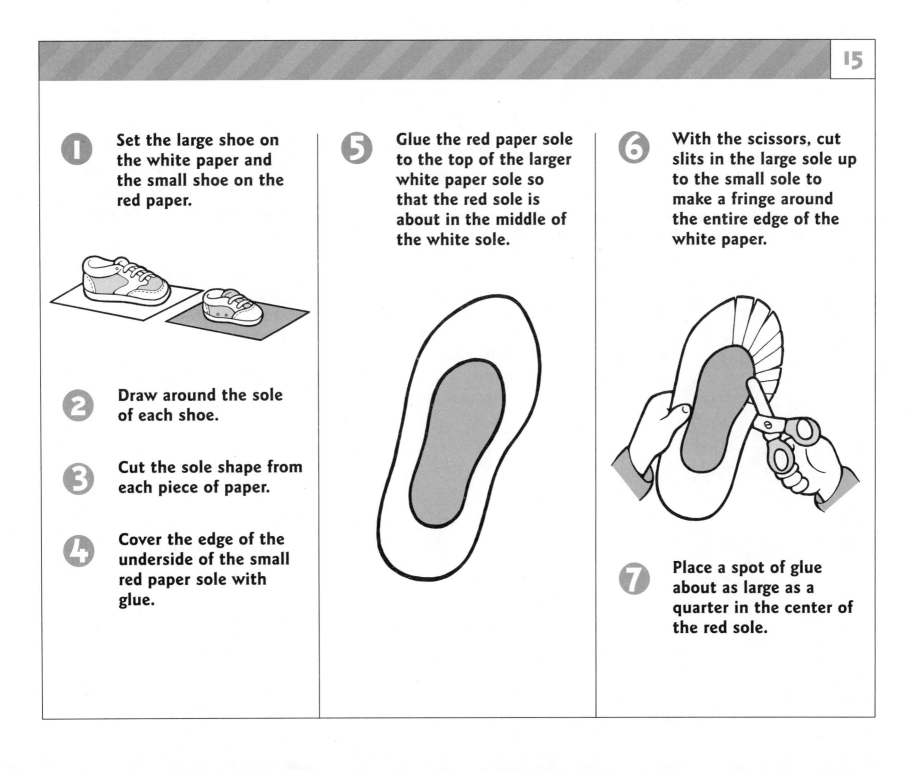

1 Set the large shoe on the white paper and the small shoe on the red paper.

2 Draw around the sole of each shoe.

3 Cut the sole shape from each piece of paper.

4 Cover the edge of the underside of the small red paper sole with glue.

5 Glue the red paper sole to the top of the larger white paper sole so that the red sole is about in the middle of the white sole.

6 With the scissors, cut slits in the large sole up to the small sole to make a fringe around the entire edge of the white paper.

7 Place a spot of glue about as large as a quarter in the center of the red sole.

8 Cover the spot of glue with glitter.

9 Glue the white sole to the blue sheet of paper. Label the blue paper Paramecium.

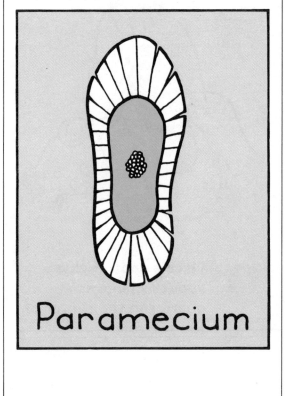

Paramecium

So Now We Know

Pond water contains some living creatures that are so small they cannot be seen without a microscope. Some of these creatures are made of only one cell. The paramecium is one such creature. This creature is often called the "slipper animal" because it looks like the sole of a shoe. It moves around by fluttering hairs that cover the outside of its body. You have made a paper model of a slipper animal. The white paper fringe represents the hairs around the paramecium. The glitter spot represents its control center.

More Fun Things to Know and Do

Another tiny critter in pond water is the euglena. It moves around by whipping a long, stringlike structure. Here's how to make a model of a euglena.

- Cut a pear shape from the yellow paper.

- Cut small, long oval shapes from the green paper and glue them around the inside edge of the pear shape. The green ovals represent the euglena's food factories.

- Place a spot of glue in the center of the larger end of the pear shape and cover the spot with glitter. As with the slipper animal, the glitter spot represents the control center of the euglena.

- Glue a string that is at least as long as the euglena to the smaller end of the pear shape.

- Glue the yellow paper to the blue paper. Label the blue paper Euglena.

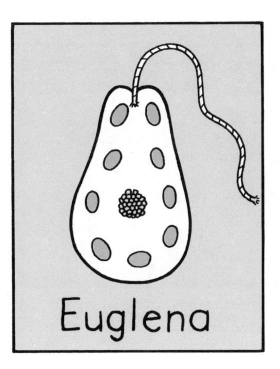

Predators and Prey

Blending

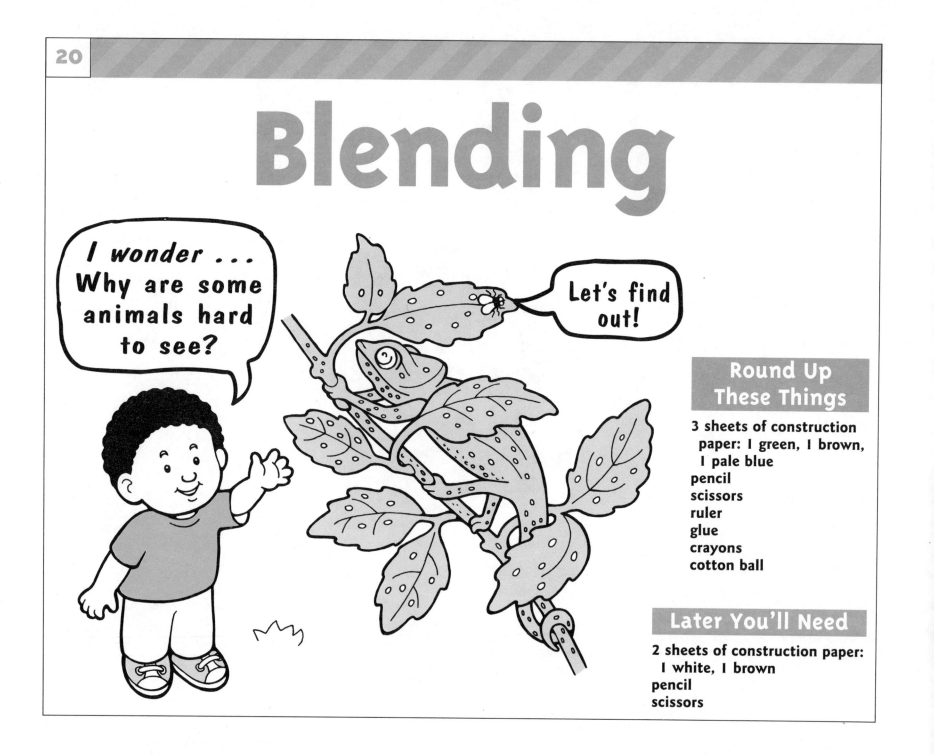

1 Lay the green paper on top of the brown paper.

2 On one of the shorter edges of the green paper, mark and cut a 2-inch (5-cm)-wide strip, making sure to cut through both sheets of paper.

3 Glue the 2 paper strips together, back to back. Set them aside and allow the glue to dry.

4 Fold what's left of the stacked sheets of green and brown paper in half lengthwise (long end to long end).

5 Draw 3 blades of grass on the folded sheets of paper as shown.

6 **ADULT STEP** Cut out each blade, making sure to cut through all four layers of paper and across the fold. You will have 6 blades of each color.

7 Place all 12 blades of grass along one of the longer edges of the blue paper. Alternate the colors, placing 3 blades of one color together as shown. Glue the blades of grass to the blue paper.

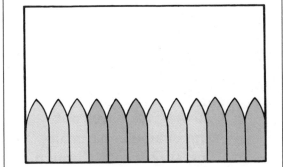

8 Complete the picture by using crayons to add a sun and birds. Separate the fibers of the cotton ball and glue it on the blue paper to represent a cloud.

9 Fold the glued strip prepared in step 3 in half lengthwise. Make a mark in the center of the strip to divide it in half. Draw two half chameleons on the fold of the strip, one on either side of the mark, as shown.

10 ADULT STEP Cut out the chameleons, making sure to cut through both thicknesses of the glued strip.

11 Place the chameleons green side up on the green grass blades. Observe how well you can see the green chameleons.

12 Turn the chameleons over, brown side up, and place them on the brown grass blades. Again observe how well you can see the brown chameleons.

13 Turn one chameleon over, green side up, and leave it on the brown grass. Which chameleon is easier to see?

So Now We Know

Some animals can change color. When an animal's color blends in with its surroundings, the animal is hard to see. This makes it hard for the animal's enemies to see it. The chameleon is a lizard that can change its skin color to different shades of green, yellow, and brown, which is the same color as the grass, branches, and soil where it lives. The paper chameleons you made were hard to see against the paper grass of the same color.

More Fun Things to Know and Do

The fur of some rabbits is white during the snowy winter months and changes to brown during the warm months. This allows the rabbit to blend in with its surroundings. Make paper rabbits and decide which would blend in with your outdoor surroundings.

- Use the papers to make one white and one brown rabbit.

- Take the rabbits outdoors and place them on different surfaces. Decide which rabbit blends in better with your outdoor surroundings.

- Test them again later when the season changes and your outdoor surroundings change.

Bright Eyes

Round Up
These Things

chalk
ruler
black construction paper
scissors
empty coffee can (inside
  bottom must be shiny)
rubber band
flashlight

Later You'll Need

mirror
timer

1 With the chalk, draw an oval about 3 inches (7.5 cm) long and 1 inch (2.5 cm) wide in the center of the paper.

2 Cut the oval out of the paper. Discard the oval cutout.

3 Place the paper over the open end of the can so that the oval hole in the paper is in the center of the can's opening. Secure the paper to the can with the rubber band.

4 Take the can and the flashlight to a room that you can make very dark, and turn out the lights.

5 Hold the can in front of you as far away as you can at eye level so that the hole in the paper faces you.

6 Look toward the hole in the paper. You will find that it is difficult or impossible to see the hole (or even the can, if the room is very dark).

7 Hold the flashlight near your face so that the light points at the hole in the paper.

8 Look toward the hole in the paper. The light from the flashlight will reflect off the shiny bottom of the can, making the hole appear to glow.

So Now We Know

The glow from a cat's eyes is light that has entered through the opening in the eye and bounced off the shiny mirrorlike lining at the back of the eye. This special lining helps the cat see better at night so that it can more easily find food.

More Fun Things to Know and Do

The pupil is a black opening in the center of the eye of cats and other animals, such as humans. It enlarges in the dark so that more light can get into the eye. To make your pupil get larger, keep one eye open and the other eye closed. Use your hand to cover the closed eye. Observe the size of the pupil of the open eye by looking in the mirror. At the end of 2 to 3 minutes, remove your hand, open the closed eye, and look at it in the mirror. Watch what happens to the size of the pupil in the light.

Catchers

Round Up These Things

small envelope
scissors
marking pen
rubber band
small bowl of popcorn
small bowl

Later You'll Need

raisin cookie
paper plate
ballpoint pen
round toothpick

1 Open the envelope's flap.

2 Cut off the flap and part of the front (the side where the mailing address is written) so that the front matches the back.

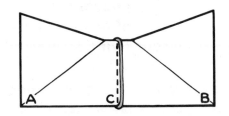

3 Fold the envelope in half widthwise (short end to short end).

4 Unfold the envelope and label the corners A and B, and the bottom edge of the envelope at the fold C.

5 Slip the rubber band around the fold.

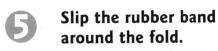

6 Open the envelope and put the hand you write with inside so that your hand is under the rubber band, your fingers point toward corner A, and your thumb points toward corner B.

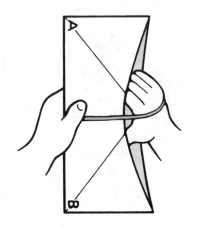

7 With your other hand, push the bottom edge of the envelope at point C toward the hand inside the envelope.

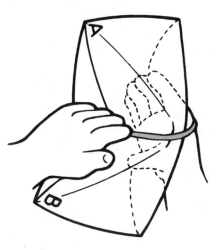

8 Use your fingers and thumb inside the envelope to fold the envelope across the bottom edge and over your other hand. You will have a model of a bird's biting beak.

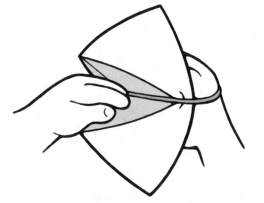

9 Open and close the beak several times so that the model stays in a beak shape.

10 Ask your helper to throw one piece of popcorn at a time into

the air. Using only your paper beak, catch the falling popcorn. The pieces of popcorn represent flying insects.

11 Place the pieces of popcorn that you catch in a bowl and count them when you're done. How many "insects" did you catch? Was it difficult to catch them?

12 Repeat steps 10 and 11 while you toss the popcorn and your helper holds the beak.

So Now We Know

The shape and size of a bird's beak and mouth help it to catch food. Some birds have very large, gaping mouths with which to catch flying insects. Your large paper beak helped you catch at least some pieces of tossed popcorn.

More Fun Things to Know and Do

Woodpeckers have hard, flat bills (beaks) and long, swordlike tongues. The bill is used to dig insects out of wood, and the tongue is used to spear the exposed insects. A pen and toothpick can be used to represent the bill and tongue of a woodpecker. A raisin cookie can represent a tree with the raisins as the insects. Place the cookie on the paper plate and use the pointed end of the pen to dig pieces of the cookie from around a raisin. Use the toothpick to spear the raisin and remove it from the cookie. *CAUTION: Do not eat the raisins or the pieces of the cookie. Throw the cookie away after the experiment.*

Snare

I wonder ... Why don't spiders get caught in their own webs?

Let's find out!

Round Up These Things

transparent tape
ruler
sheet of black construction
  paper
pencil

Later You'll Need

model from the original
  experiment
          plus
cooking oil
hair spray
baby powder
dark construction paper
scissors

1 Tear off a piece of tape 4 to 6 inches (10 to 15 cm) long. Stick the tape across the center of the paper.

2 Tear off a piece of tape the same length as the first and cross it over the first piece of tape.

3 Tear off 2 more pieces of tape the same length as the others and cross them over the other pieces as shown in the diagram.

4 With your pointer finger, tap along the surface of each piece of tape on the paper. Observe what happens to your finger.

5 Tear off a fifth piece of tape the same length as the others and lay it sticky side up across the other pieces of tape. Turn the edges of the tape under so it sticks to the paper.

6 Use the eraser of the pencil to tap along the surface of the sticky piece of tape. Observe what happens to the eraser.

So Now We Know

Spiderwebs are made of sticky and nonsticky strands. The parts of the web made of nonsticky strands look like the spokes of a wheel. The first 4 pieces of tape in your model represent the support strands of a spiderweb. Your finger represents the leg of a spider. Spiders do not stick to the web if they walk along the nonsticky support strands. The strands that spiral between the spokes of the spiderweb are covered with a sticky substance like the fifth piece of tape in your model. When an insect flies into the spiderweb, its legs, like the eraser of the pencil, gets caught in the sticky strands.

More Fun Things to Know and Do

1 Spiders rarely get caught even if they walk on the sticky strands, because they have oil on their feet. Wet your pointer finger with oil and touch it to the sticky tape used in the previous experiment. Your finger does not stick.

2 Spiders of the same kind build the same web shapes. Here's how to collect a spiderweb. **CAUTION:** *Be sure the spider is not in the web.*

- Make the web stickier by spraying it with hair spray.

- Quickly blow some baby powder over the sticky web by squeezing the powder container.

- Spray the paper with hair spray and push the sticky side of the paper against the web.

- Hold the paper in place while your adult helper cuts the web's support strands.

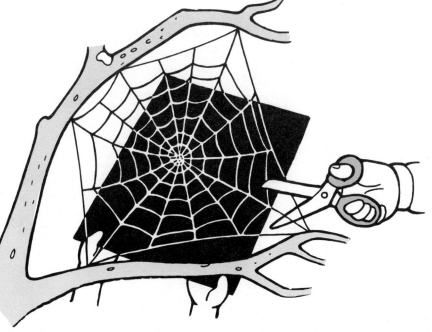

Body Temperature

Chill Out

Round Up These Things

small bowl
tap water
cotton ball
ruler

Later You'll Need

the same materials
plus
bulb-type thermometer
timer

1 Fill the bowl about half full with water.

2 Dip the cotton ball into the water in the bowl and squeeze out any excess water.

3 Rub the wet cotton ball over the surface of your arm.

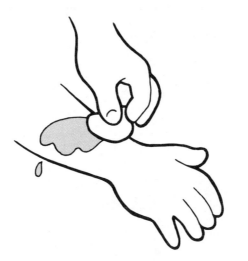

4 Hold your wet arm about 4 inches (10 cm) from your mouth.

5 Blow across the wet area on your arm. How does your arm feel?

So Now We Know

A dog does not sweat like you do when it gets hot. Instead, it pants by blowing its breath over its wet tongue. This helps the dog cool off, just as your arm felt cooler after you wet it and blew your breath across it.

More Fun Things to Know and Do

A thermometer is an instrument that measures changes in temperature. Let's use a thermometer to show the change in temperature that happens when you blow on something wet.

- Lay the thermometer on a table. Observe the level of the liquid line in the thermometer.

- Moisten the cotton ball with water. Separate the fibers of the cotton ball and lay a thin layer of wet cotton across the bulb of the thermometer.

- Keeping your mouth about 4 inches (10 cm) away from the wet cotton, blow your breath across the wet cotton about 15 times. Observe the level of the liquid line in the thermometer again. If the line goes up, it indicates an increase in temperature. If the line goes down, it indicates a decrease in temperature.

Overcoats

I wonder ... How do animals stay warm in the winter?

Let's find out!

Round Up These Things

wool glove
2 ice cubes

Later You'll Need

1 tablespoon (15 ml) vegetable
  shortening
two 1-quart (1-liter) plastic
  bags
2 ice cubes

1 Put the glove on your hand.

2 Hold one ice cube in the gloved hand and the other ice cube in your other hand for about 5 seconds. Measure 5 seconds by counting to 5, saying "one thousand" before each number (one thousand one, one thousand two, and so on). Notice how cold the ice makes each hand feel.

So Now We Know

Animals don't have overcoats to put on when it is cold. Instead they have a permanent coat of fur or feathers that they wear all year long. The coat gets thicker during the winter. The wool glove, like the fur or feathers on an animal, protects against the cold. The skin on your hand, like the skin on an animal, is a waterproof covering but doesn't offer much protection against the cold.

More Fun Things to Know and Do

Some animals that live in very cold places, such as walruses, seals, and whales, have a thick layer of blubber (fat) under their skin. Let's see how this fatty layer helps to keep them warm.

- Place the shortening in your left hand.

- Place your hand inside the bag. The plastic bag represents the skin on an animal, and the shortening represents the layer of fat beneath the skin.

- Place your other hand inside the other plastic bag. Cup your hand and place the other ice cube on top of this plastic bag.

- Hold the ice in your hands for about 5 seconds. Compare how cold each hand feels.

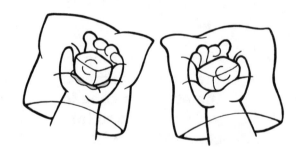

- Cup your shortening-covered hand and place the ice cube on top of the plastic bag.

Animal Movement

Glider

**Round Up
These Things**

sheet of typing paper
marking pen
scissors
2 paper clips

Later You'll Need

the same materials

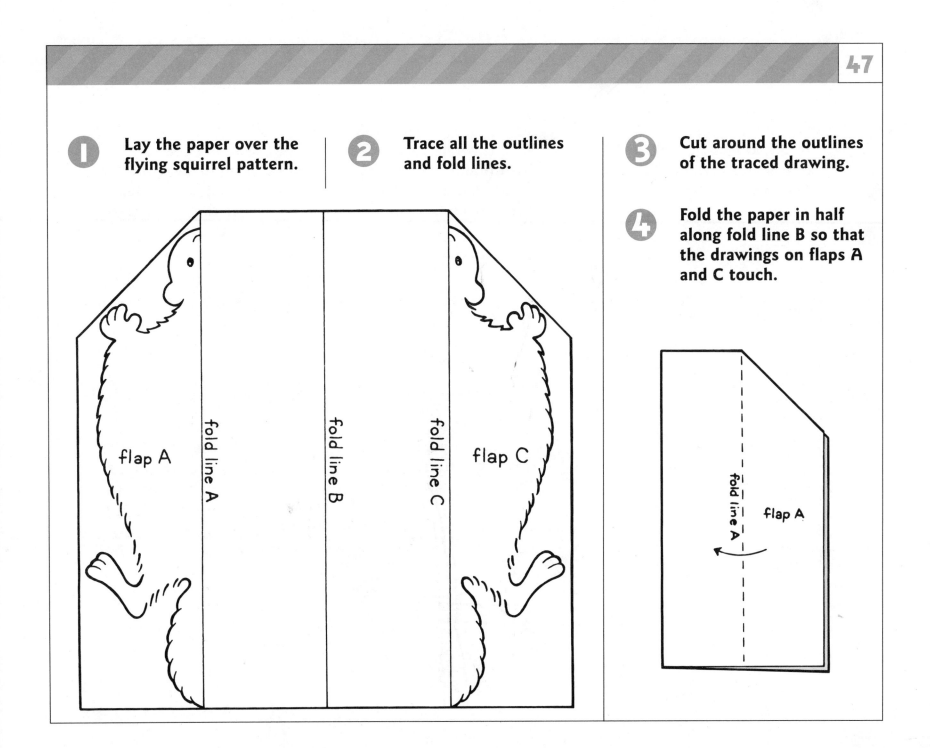

1. Lay the paper over the flying squirrel pattern.

2. Trace all the outlines and fold lines.

3. Cut around the outlines of the traced drawing.

4. Fold the paper in half along fold line B so that the drawings on flaps A and C touch.

flap A

fold line A

fold line B

fold line C

flap C

fold line A

flap A

5 Fold flap A along fold line A and toward the first fold.

6 Turn the paper over, then fold flap C along fold line C and toward the first fold.

8 Holding the squirrel from below (fold line B), adjust the flaps so that they are parallel to the ground.

9 Throw the squirrel to make it glide through the air.

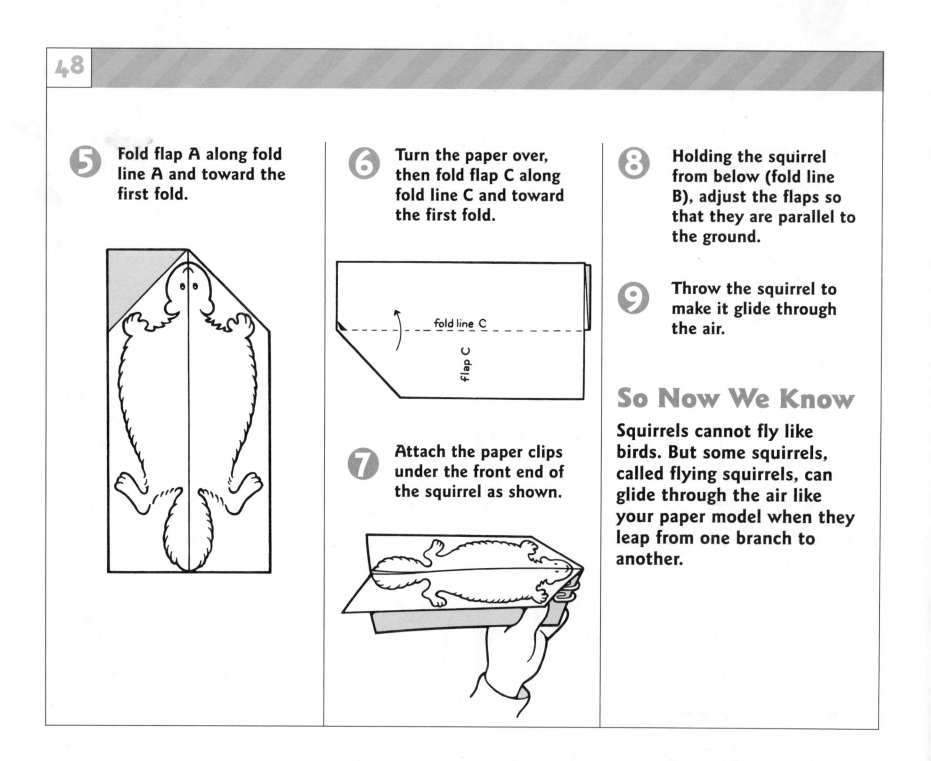

fold line C

flap C

7 Attach the paper clips under the front end of the squirrel as shown.

So Now We Know

Squirrels cannot fly like birds. But some squirrels, called flying squirrels, can glide through the air like your paper model when they leap from one branch to another.

More Fun Things to Know and Do

Lizards in the rain forest of Asia, called flying dragons, also have extra flaps of skin along the sides of their bodies. The flying dragon, like the flying squirrel, is able to glide through the air for short distances. Repeat the experiment, replacing the flying squirrel pattern with that of the flying dragon as shown.

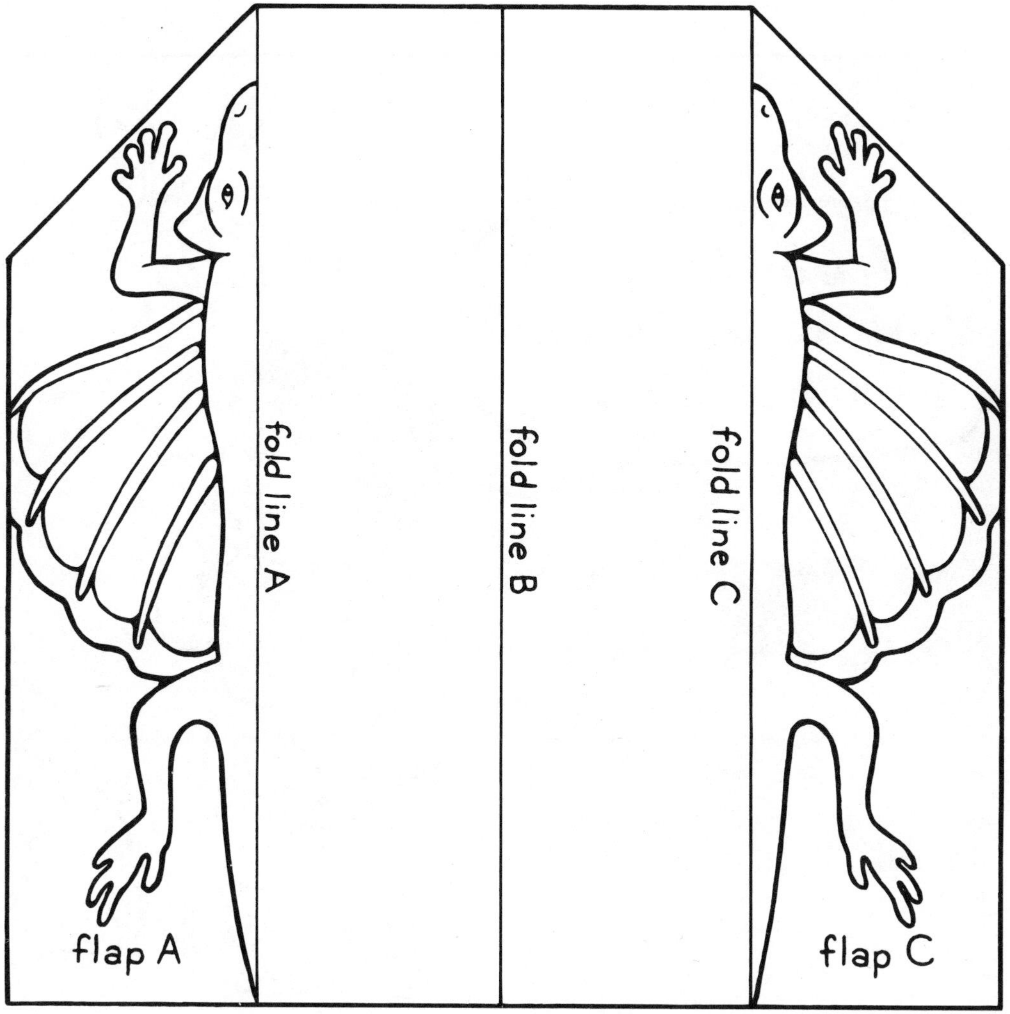

fold line A

fold line B

fold line C

flap A

flap C

Stand with your feet about 12 inches (30 cm) apart and your hands to your sides.

Bend your left knee so that your left foot is lifted about 4 inches (10 cm) above the floor. Notice how your body leans toward the right.

Return your foot to the floor and move next to the wall.

4 Stand as before, with your feet about 12 inches (30 cm) apart, placing your right foot and right shoulder against the wall.

5 Try to bend your left knee as before so that your left foot is lifted about 4 inches (10 cm) above the floor. Observe what happens.

So Now We Know

A bird or any animal that walks on two legs leans one way or the other when lifting its legs to walk. If the bird can't lean, as you couldn't when you stood next to the wall, it will fall over if it raises its foot.

More Fun Things to Know and Do

In order to balance while walking, a four-legged animal generally must have three feet on the ground. Three legs support the weight of the body while the fourth leg swings forward to a new position. One leg after the other is lifted in a certain order. To move in the same pattern as do sheep, horses, or dogs, try this:

- Get on your hands and knees. Your hands and knees will be your "feet."

- Crawl slowly, moving your "feet" forward one at a time in this order: right front, left rear, left front, right rear.

- Four-legged animals can balance on two feet when they are walking fast or running. They move their legs in a certain order. To move your "feet" in this order try this: Crawl by moving your right front "foot" and left rear "foot" forward at the same time. Then move your left front "foot" and right rear" foot" forward.

Floaters

Round Up These Things

large bowl
tap water
2 glass marbles
two 7-inch (17.5-cm)
  round balloons

Later You'll Need

4 to 5 fast-food condiment
  packets (ketchup, mayon-
  naise, soy sauce, etc.)
1-quart (1-liter) jar
tap water
2-liter plastic soda bottle
  with cap

1 Fill the bowl about three-fourths full with water.

2 Place 1 marble inside each balloon.

3 In one of the balloons, tie a knot as close to the marble as possible.

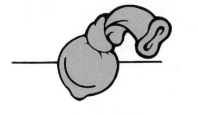

4 Slightly inflate the second balloon, and tie a knot as close to the mouth of the balloon as possible.

5 Drop both of the balloons in the bowl of water. The inflated balloon will float on the surface of the water, but the deflated balloon will sink to the bottom of the bowl.

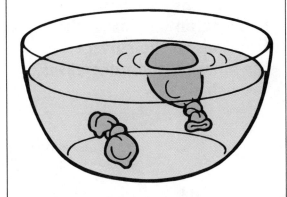

So Now We Know

Fish do not have marbles inside them. The marble is used to make the balloon heavy. Fish do have a special organ inside them that works like a balloon. Like the ballons in the experiment, as the amount of air inside the fish's organ increases, the fish rises to the surface. As the amount of air decreases, the fish sinks.

More Fun Things to Know and Do

Here is another way to demonstrate the rising and sinking of a fish.

- Decide which of the condiment packets will make the best model of a fish. Do this by filling the jar about three-fourths full with water and dropping all of the packets into the water. The best fish model is the packet that just barely sinks below the water's surface.

- **Fill the soda bottle to overflowing with water.**

- **Insert the selected condiment packet in the bottle. Add water if necessary so that the bottle is still overflowing with water.**

- **Secure the cap on the bottle.**

- **Squeeze the bottle with your hands. The air bubble in the packet will shrink and the model fish will sink.**

- **Release the pressure on the bottle. The air bubble inside the packet will get bigger and the model fish will rise.**

Squirters

Round Up These Things

12-inch (30-cm) round balloon

Later You'll Need

scissors
ruler
12 feet (360 cm) curling ribbon (any color)
umbrella
transparent tape

1 Inflate the balloon and hold the mouth of the balloon shut between your fingers.

2 Release the balloon. The balloon will move around as it deflates.

So Now We Know

Like the balloon that jets through the air around it as it deflates, an octopus jets through the water in the ocean. The octopus sucks in water and squirts it out through an opening under its head. The force of the water leaving the octopus moves the animal forward.

More Fun Things to Know and Do

Jellyfish also move by pushing out water. They are shaped much like an open umbrella from which long streamers hang down. Their open bodies fill with water. They can move up through the water by closing their bodies, which pushes the water out. Use an umbrella to demonstrate the movement of jellyfish.

- Cut the ribbon into eight 18-inch (45-cm) strips.

- Open the umbrella and lay it upside down on a table

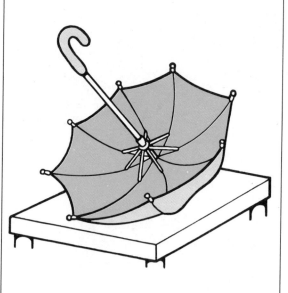

- **Use tape to secure the long strips of ribbon to the tip of each rib of the umbrella.**

- **Open and close the umbrella and watch the movement of the ribbons and the umbrella.**

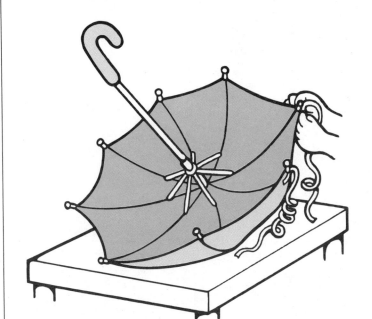

Plant
Growth

Baby Plants

1 Fill the glass half full with water.

2 Put the beans in the glass of water to soften their outer coverings.

3 Set the glass of beans in a refrigerator overnight. Keeping the beans cool prevents bacteria from growing and making the beans sour.

4 Remove the beans from the water and place them on the paper towel to dry.

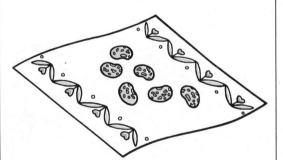

5 With your fingernail, scratch off the outer covering of one of the beans.

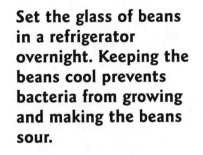

6 Holding the bean in your hands, pry the two parts of the bean apart with your fingers.

7 Shine the light from the flashlight on the bean as you observe the inside of the bean with the magnifying lens. A tiny, colorless, plantlike structure with two leaves will be stuck to one of the bean parts.

8 Repeat steps 5 and 6 with the other beans.

So Now We Know

Inside each bean is a structure that looks like a baby plant. This structure is called the embryo.

More Fun Things to Know and Do

The embryo is easy to find in large seeds. Repeat the experiment using other beans, such as lima or kidney beans.

Anywhere?

I wonder ... How can grass grow in a sidewalk?

Let's find out!

Round Up These Things

9-ounce (270-ml) paper cup
cotton balls
1 cup (250 ml) tap water
½ teaspoon (2.5 ml) rye, Bermuda, Johnson, or other grass seed (purchased or collected from grass plants)

Later You'll Need

two 5-ounce (150-ml) paper cups
potting soil
2 teaspoons (10 ml) rye, Bermuda, Johnson, or other grass seed
1-teaspoon (5-ml) measuring spoon
tap water
dishwashing sponge

1 Fill the cup with cotton balls.

2 Add water to the cup until the cotton is totally wet.

3 Pour the grass seed into the palm of your hand. Picking up a few seeds at a time, sprinkle them evenly over the cotton.

4 Place the cup in a window that receives sunlight at least part of the day. The light from the sun will keep the soil warm.

5 Keep the cotton moist during the experiment.

6 Observe the cotton daily for 2 weeks or until the grass stops growing. The seeds will grow, forming a layer of green grass on the cotton.

So Now We Know

Grass seeds only need warmth, light, water, and air to grow into green grass. Grass is often found growing in unusual places, such as the cracks of sidewalks and driveways. The grass seed is blown by the wind or washed by water into these cracks. Usually there is a small amount of soil in the cracks, but the seeds don't need the soil to start growing.

More Fun Things to Know and Do

Grass seeds will develop into plants with or without light if they have warmth, water, air, and food, such as found in the soil, but the grass needs light in order to be green and healthy. Here's a way to show this.

- Fill the paper cups half full with potting soil

- Sprinkle ½ teaspoon (2.5 ml) of seeds over the surface of the soil in each cup.

- Cover the seeds in each cup with 3 teaspoons (15 ml) of soil.

- Place one of the cups near a window and the

other cup in a dark place, such as a closet or cabinet.

- Keep the soil in both cups moist during the experiment. Whenever the soil starts to feel dry, add water by squeezing a wet sponge over the soil.

- Observe the cups daily for 2 or more weeks or until no further growth is observed. To limit the amount of light reaching the cup in the dark place, open the cabinet door just enough to see the cup's contents, then quickly close the door.

- Compare the color and height of the grass grown with light to that grown without light.

Sprouters

Round Up These Things

large 1-tablespoon (15-ml) measuring spoon
12-ounce (260-ml) paper cup
potting soil
5 dry beans, such as pinto or lima
pencil
saucer
tap water

Later You'll Need

paper towels
10-ounce (300-ml) clear plastic cup
tap water
seeds from the kitchen, such as popcorn, dill, celery, mustard, peppercorns, fennel, or whole cloves
masking tape
marking pen

1 Use the spoon to fill the paper cup three-fourths full with soil.

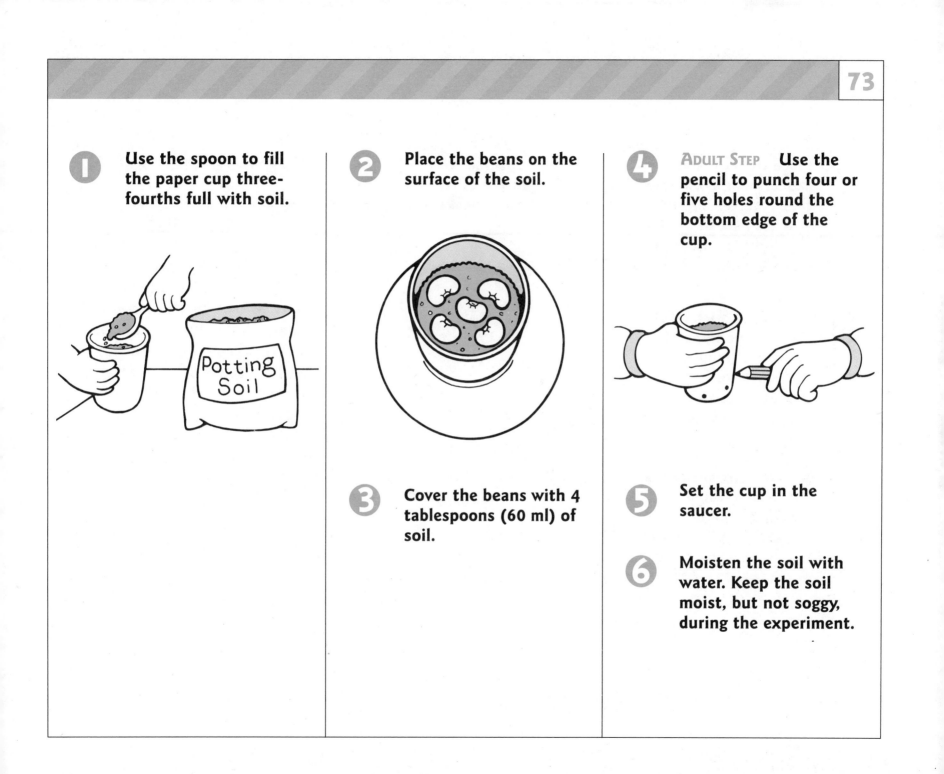

2 Place the beans on the surface of the soil.

3 Cover the beans with 4 tablespoons (60 ml) of soil.

4 ADULT STEP Use the pencil to punch four or five holes round the bottom edge of the cup.

5 Set the cup in the saucer.

6 Moisten the soil with water. Keep the soil moist, but not soggy, during the experiment.

7 Place the cup and saucer near a window that receives sunlight at least part of the day. The light from the sun will keep the soil warm.

8 Watch the surface of the soil for signs of growth. It may take 4 to 6 days for the sprouting beans to break through the soil. Look first for a hook-shaped stem to break through the surface. As the hook straightens, leaves on the end of the stem will be lifted up.

9 Continue to watch the growth of the beans for 2 to 3 weeks or longer.

So Now We Know

The dry beans in your kitchen are the seeds of a bean plant. The beans will grow if they are planted and given the right amount of light, water, air, and warmth. Beans that have been cooked will not grow because the heat kills the seed. Sometimes a bean doesn't grow because an injury has caused some of its parts to be damaged or missing.

More Fun Things to Know and Do

Not all of the seeds that you find in your kitchen will grow. Many have been heated or injured in other ways. Plant other seeds found in the kitchen to see whether they will grow.

- Prepare a see-through growing cup by folding a paper towel in half and lining the inside of the plastic cup with it.

- Crumple other paper towels and stuff them into the cup to hold the paper lining tightly against the sides of the cup.

- Moisten the paper lining with water. Keep the lining moist, but not soggy, during the experiment.

- Take a few of one kind of seed and slip each seed between the paper lining and the cup. Leave space between the seeds, but group seeds of the same type in one section of the cup.

- Take a few of another kind of seed and slip each seed between the paper lining and the cup in another section of the cup.

- Place a strip of tape around the outside of the cup. Write the name of each kind of seed on the tape.

- See which of your seeds will grow.

1 Place a small piece of tape on either side of the flowerpot.

2 Mark a dot on one piece of tape and an X on the other piece.

3 Set the plant near a window that receives direct sunlight. Turn the pot so that the X faces the window.

4 Observe the direction of the leaves every day for 1 week or longer. *NOTE: Water the plant as usual.*

5 Repeat steps 3 and 4, turning the pot so that the dot on the tape faces the window. Notice any change in the direction of the leaves.

So Now We Know

The leaves on the plant move toward the window. When the plant is turned around, the leaves again move toward the window. This happens because the plant's stems grow toward the light. As the plant stems grow, the leaves are turned toward the light.

More Fun Things to Know and Do

I wonder . . . Does a sunflower always face the sun?

Sunflowers face the sun during the day. To do this, they turn during the day to follow the sun from east to west. Observe this by doing the following:

- Find a sunflower growing outdoors.

- Several times during the day, use the compass to determine the direction that the sunflower is facing. *CAUTION: Do not look at the sun. It can damage your eyes.*

Plant
Parts

Thirsty Plant

I wonder . . . How do plants get a drink of water?

Let's find out!

Round Up These Things

drinking glass
tap water
red food coloring
spoon
scissors
fresh stalk of celery with leaves (preferably the pale innermost stalk)

Later You'll Need

the same materials
plus
ruler
magnifying lens
long-stemmed white carnation

1 Fill the glass about one-fourth full with water.

2 Add 10 drops of food coloring. Stir.

3 Use the scissors to cut across the bottom end of the celery stalk.

4 Stand the stalk in the glass of colored water so that the cut end is underwater.

5 Observe the leaves as often as possible for 2 days. *NOTE: Keep the celery stalk for the first experiment in "More Fun Things to Know and Do."*

So Now We Know

Plants get most of their water from the ground. The water enters the plant through the roots and moves through tiny tubes in the stem to the leaves and other plant parts. You could not see the colored water moving through the celery stalk, but you could see the change of color in the leaves.

More Fun Things to Know and Do

The red food coloring in the water stains the tubes that run throughout the plant. The red-stained tubes can be seen as small dots around the

flat end of a section of the stalk. Use the scissors to cut a small section about 1 inch (2.25 cm) long from the celery stalk used in the experiment. Study the inside of the celery section with the magnifying lens. Notice the row of tiny red dots around the flat end of the section.

Colored water can also be used to change the color of a flower.

- Fill the glass one-fourth full with water.

- Add 10 drops of food coloring. Stir.

- Use the scissors to cut across the bottom of the stem of the carnation.

- Stand the flower in the glass of colored water.

- Observe the flower's color as often as possible for 2 days. Notice the streaks of color that appear in the petals.

Juicy

Round Up These Things

manila file folder
ruler
transparent tape
1-gallon (4-liter) plastic
  produce bag
1-quart (1-liter) pitcher
tap water

Later You'll Need

scissors
dishwashing sponge
2 saucers
petroleum jelly
½ cup (125 ml) tap water

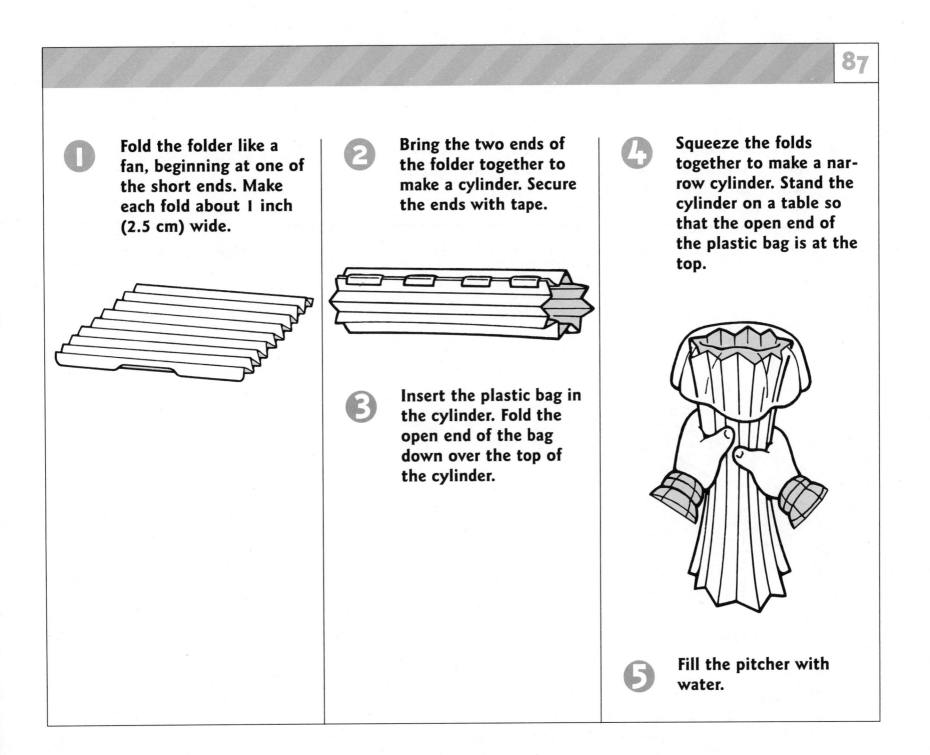

1 Fold the folder like a fan, beginning at one of the short ends. Make each fold about 1 inch (2.5 cm) wide.

2 Bring the two ends of the folder together to make a cylinder. Secure the ends with tape.

3 Insert the plastic bag in the cylinder. Fold the open end of the bag down over the top of the cylinder.

4 Squeeze the folds together to make a narrow cylinder. Stand the cylinder on a table so that the open end of the plastic bag is at the top.

5 Fill the pitcher with water.

6 Hold the cylinder upright on the table as your helper slowly pours the water from the pitcher into the plastic bag.

7 Observe the cylinder as the water enters the bag.

So Now We Know

The outsides of some cacti are pleated like the cylinder. This allows them to swell with water during rainy periods, just as your cylinder swelled with water. This water is used by the cactus when it doesn't rain.

More Fun Things to Know and Do

All plants lose water through their leaves and stems. The leaves of many desert plants have a thick, waxy coat. See how this coat makes it harder for the plants to lose water.

- **ADULT STEP** Cut the sponge in half.

- Lay one half of the sponge in one of the saucers.

- Cover all but one of the larger surfaces of the other half of the sponge with a thick layer of petroleum jelly.

- Lay the greased sponge, ungreased side down, in the second saucer.

- Pour half of the water into each saucer. When both sponges have soaked up the water, pour out the excess water from the saucers.

- Once a day, touch the undersides of the sponge pieces to see whether they are wet. How long does it take them to dry? Which sponge dries out first?

Plant Paints

I wonder ...
How does the
green in grass get
on my clothes?

Round Up These Things

grass
paper plate
sheet of typing paper

Later You'll Need

4 to 6 sheets of newspaper
white cotton T-shirt
cutting board
10 to 12 brightly colored flower
 petals, yellow or red
4 to 6 leaves
6-inch (15-cm)-square sheet of
 waxed paper
lemon-size rock

Let's find
out!

1 Break off enough blades of grass to cover the bottom of the paper plate.

2 Set the plate of grass on a hard surface, such as a sidewalk or floor.

3 Cover the grass in the plate with the paper.

4 Step on the paper and twist the ball of your foot to crush the grass without tearing the paper.

5 Lift the paper and look at it. You will see green on the paper where the coloring substance from the crushed grass stained the paper.

So Now We Know

The green color in grass comes from a coloring substance in the plant called chlorophyll. Normally, the chlorophyll stays inside the grass. When you play on grass, the grass gets crushed. Then the chlorophyll can get out and stain your clothes green.

More Fun Things to Know and Do

Plant parts, such as leaves and flowers, contain coloring substances. Leaves are usually green, but flowers vary greatly in color. If plant parts are crushed, their coloring substance, like that in grass, can get out and stain cloth. Use plant parts to create a flower design on the front of a T-shirt.

- Fold the newspaper and place it inside the shirt.

- Lay the shirt on the cutting board so that the front of the shirt is face-up.

- Arrange the flower petals and leaves in the center of the shirt front. Make small piles of petals and leaves to form a design.

- Cover the flower parts with the waxed paper.

- Crush the petals and leaves by tapping them

with the rock so that their coloring substance can get out. *CAUTION: Hold the rock in one hand and keep the other hand away so you do not hit your fingers.*

- Remove the waxed paper and crushed petals and leaves. *NOTE: Washing the shirt by hand in cold water will help keep the colors bright.*

Browning

I wonder . . . Why do peeled bananas turn brown?

Let's find out!

Round Up These Things

2 bananas
paper plate
butter knife

Later You'll Need

chewable vitamin C tablet
paper towel
rolling pin
paring knife (to be used only by
  an adult)
apple
2 paper plates
lemon
timer

1 Peel one banana and place it on the paper plate.

2 Use the butter knife to cut the banana into four sections.

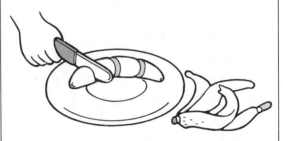

3 Look at the banana slices as often as possible during the day. You will find that the outside of each banana slice slowly turns darker.

4 After 4 to 5 hours or longer, peel the second banana and use the butter knife to cut it into four sections.

5 Compare the color of the two sectioned bananas.

So Now We Know

Bananas are protected by their skins. When the skin is peeled off, air touches the banana and it turns brown.

More Fun Things to Know and Do

Other fruits, such as apples and pears, also turn dark when their protective skin is broken or removed. Vitamin C can be used to help keep the fruit from turning dark.

- Wrap the vitamin C tablet in the paper towel and crush it by rolling the rolling pin back and forth across the towel.

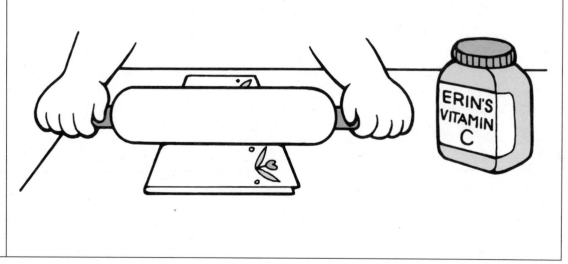

ERIN'S VITAMIN C

- ADULT STEP Use the paring knife to cut an unpeeled apple in half. Place the sections on separate plates.

- ADULT STEP Cut one of the sections in half.

- Sprinkle the crushed vitamin C tablet over the surface of one of the smaller sections.

- ADULT STEP Cut the lemon in half.

- Squeeze the juice from one of the lemon halves over the surface of the second small section. *NOTE: Lemons contain Vitamin C.*

- Compare the color of the surfaces of the three apple sections after they have been exposed to the air for one hour or more.

Flowers

Guides

I wonder ... Why do bees like flowers?

Let's find out!

Round Up These Things

sheet of tracing paper
pencil
scissors
2 sheets of construction paper:
  1 red, 1 green
black marking pen
flexible straw
stick of modeling clay
one-hole paper punch
transparent tape
2-inch (5-cm) piece of green
  pipe cleaner
six 3-inch (7.5-cm) pieces of
  yellow pipe cleaners

Later You'll Need

model from the original experiment
plus
¼ teaspoon (63 ml) fine-ground yellow
  corn meal
three 2-inch (5-cm) pieces of black or
  any dark color pipe cleaners
pencil

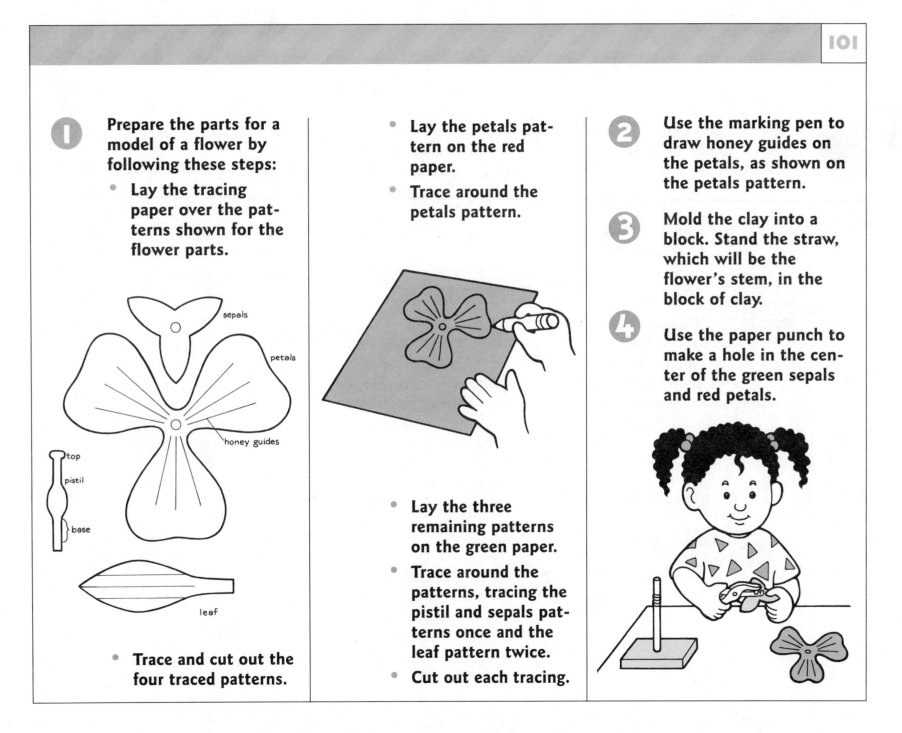

1 Prepare the parts for a model of a flower by following these steps:

- Lay the tracing paper over the patterns shown for the flower parts.

sepals

petals

honey guides

top

pistil

base

leaf

- Trace and cut out the four traced patterns.

- Lay the petals pattern on the red paper.
- Trace around the petals pattern.

- Lay the three remaining patterns on the green paper.
- Trace around the patterns, tracing the pistil and sepals patterns once and the leaf pattern twice.
- Cut out each tracing.

2 Use the marking pen to draw honey guides on the petals, as shown on the petals pattern.

3 Mold the clay into a block. Stand the straw, which will be the flower's stem, in the block of clay.

4 Use the paper punch to make a hole in the center of the green sepals and red petals.

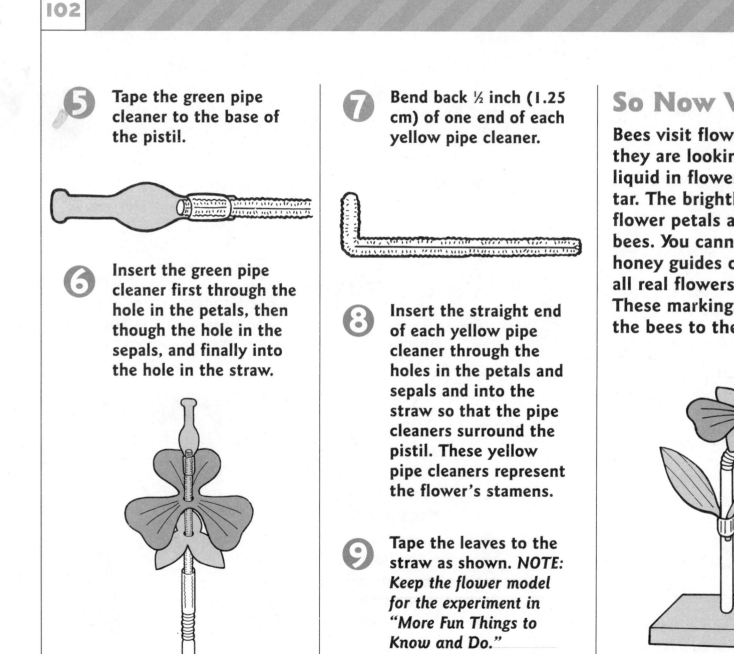

5 Tape the green pipe cleaner to the base of the pistil.

6 Insert the green pipe cleaner first through the hole in the petals, then though the hole in the sepals, and finally into the hole in the straw.

7 Bend back ½ inch (1.25 cm) of one end of each yellow pipe cleaner.

8 Insert the straight end of each yellow pipe cleaner through the holes in the petals and sepals and into the straw so that the pipe cleaners surround the pistil. These yellow pipe cleaners represent the flower's stamens.

9 Tape the leaves to the straw as shown. *NOTE: Keep the flower model for the experiment in "More Fun Things to Know and Do."*

So Now We Know

Bees visit flowers because they are looking for a sugary liquid in flowers called nectar. The brightly colored flower petals attract the bees. You cannot see the honey guides on the petals of all real flowers but bees can. These markings help guide the bees to the nectar.

More Fun Things to Know and Do

The stamens of flowers make a yellow dust called pollen. The pollen sticks to the hairy legs of bees when they touch the flower. When the bee moves around on the flower or flies to another flower, some of the pollen is dropped onto the flower's pistil. When this happens, the flower can make a seed. Here's how this happens.

- Sprinkle the corn meal on the stamens of the flower made in the experiment. The corn meal represents pollen.

- Wrap the pipe cleaners around the pointed end of the pencil to form the legs and feet of a bee.

- Holding the eraser end of the pencil, touch the bee's feet and legs to the top of the pollen-covered stamens.

- Look at the feet and legs for pollen.

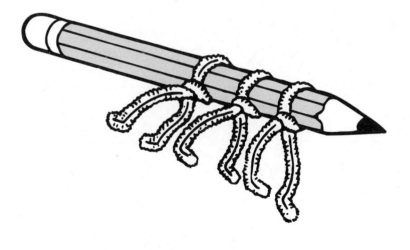

1 Lay the paper over the flower pattern and trace the flower with the pencil.

2 Cut the pattern from the paper.

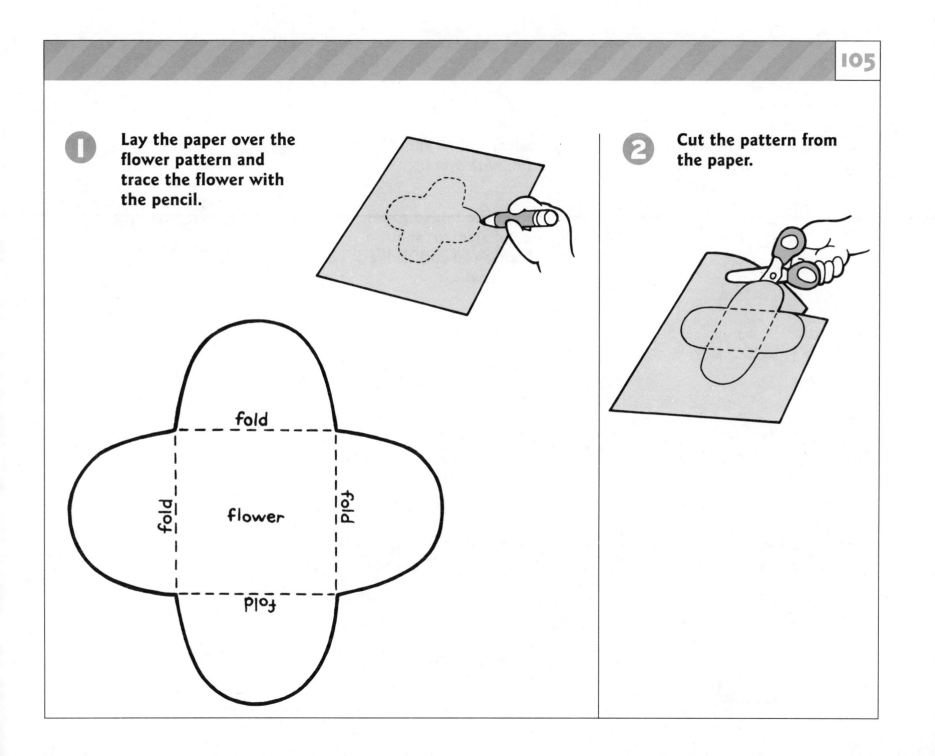

fold

fold

flower

fold

fold

3 Fold each petal toward the middle of the pattern along the fold lines.

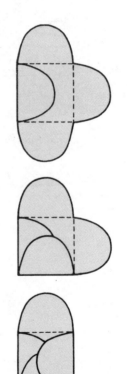

4 Fill the bowl about half full with water.

5 Hold the folded paper, petal side up, about 4 inches (10 cm) above the bowl.

6 Drop the paper into the bowl and watch the petals open.

So Now We Know

Some flowers, such as morning glories, open every morning because they fill up with a watery liquid called sap. Special tubes in the plant carry the sap from the roots to the leaves and flowers. As the flowers fill up, their petals open.

More Fun Things to Know and Do

1 Flowers have different numbers of petals. Repeat the previous experiment, making a flower with 6 petals, using the pattern shown. Does having more petals slow down the flower's opening? more slowly than others. Which paper flower opens the slowest?

2 Water moves more slowly through some types of paper and some types of flowers. Repeat the experiment, designing your own flower shape using different kinds of paper, such as newspaper and construction paper, to show how some flower petals open

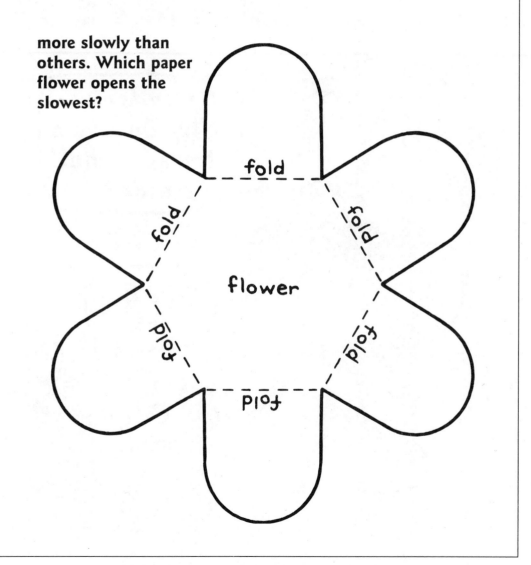

Scented

I wonder . . . Why do some flowers smell nice?

Let's find out!

Round Up These Things

baby food jar (or any small jar) with lid

2 cups (500 ml) petals of roses or other scented flower (collected from garden plants)

rubbing alcohol (to be used only by an adult)

NOTE: Get an adult's permission before collecting flower petals.

Later You'll Need

the remaining petals from the original experiment

plus

12-inch (30-cm)-square piece of netting

rubber band

1-yard (1-m) string

1 Fill the jar with the flower petals. *NOTE: Keep the remaining flower petals for the experiment in "More Fun Things to Know and Do."*

2 ADULT STEP   Fill the jar with the rubbing alcohol. Secure the lid.

Set the jar aside for 7 or more days.

4 After 7 or more days, open the jar. With your finger, dab a few drops of the liquid on your wrist. *CAUTION: Keep the alcohol away from your nose and mouth.*

5 Allow the liquid to dry, then smell your wrist.

So Now We Know

Flowers smell nice because of oils in their petals. The sweet-smelling oils in the flower petals dissolved in the alcohol. When you dabbed the liquid on your skin, the alcohol evaporated, leaving a pleasant scent on your skin.

More Fun Things to Know and Do

The smell of scented oils in flower petals attracts bees and other insects to the flower. Show how scented flowers attract insects.
NOTE: This experiment works best during warm seasons.

- Pour the flower petals remaining from the experiment into the center of the netting.

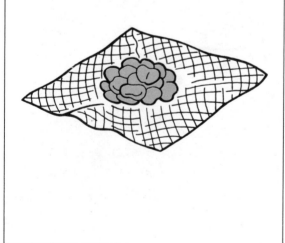

- Wrap the netting around the petals, forming a bag of petals. Secure the bag with the rubber band.

- Tie one end of the string around the top of the bag of petals to close the bag.

- Choose an outdoor place visible through a window from which you can make frequent observations of the bag. This could be a tree limb out-side a window near the kitchen table or your desk, or if no tree limb is available, the window frame itself.

- **ADULT STEP** Hang the bag of petals in the chosen spot.

- Observe the bag of petals for 2 or more days. Use an insect field guide to help you iden-tify the insects that visit the bag.

- At the end of the exper-iment, the bag of petals can be hung in your room to give the room a sweet smell. *CAUTION: Make sure there aren't any insects still on or in the bag before you bring it indoors.*

Keepers

I wonder . . . How could I keep a flower?

Let's find out!

Round Up These Things

6-inch (15-cm)-square sheet of black
   construction paper
pencil
ruler
scissors
6-inch (15-cm)-square sheet of waxed paper
two 6-inch (15-cm)-square sheets of clear
   Contact paper
plant sample (flowers and leaves of a small
   flowering plant, such as four-o'clocks or
   clover)
one-hole paper punch
6-inch (15-cm) piece of string
small suction cup with hook (used to secure
   hanging crafts to windowpanes)

Later You'll Need

the same materials
but
substitute flower with petals, such as
   a sunflower, for small flowering plant
plus
permanent marker

1 Fold the black paper in half.

2 Draw a 2-by-4-inch (5-by-10-cm) rectangle on the fold.

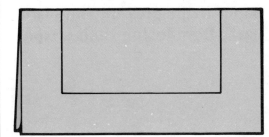

3 Cut out and discard the rectangle. Unfold the paper. You have made a frame.

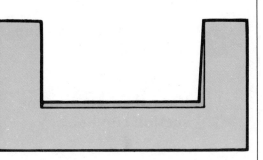

4 Place the frame on top of the waxed paper.

5 ADULT STEP Remove the backing from one piece of Contact paper and place it over the frame.

6 Turn the frame over and remove the waxed paper to expose the sticky surface of the Contact paper.

7 Arrange the flower parts on the sticky surface of the Contact paper.

8 ADULT STEP Remove the backing from the second piece of Contact paper and place it over the flowers and frame.

9 Use scissors to trim away any Contact paper that might extend past the edges of the frame.

10 Make a hole in the center top of the frame with the paper punch.

11 Thread the string through the hole in the frame and tie the ends together.

12 Attach the suction cup to a window.

13 Hang the frame on the suction cup hook.

So Now We Know

As fresh flowers and other plant parts get older, they dry and lose their shape. Sandwiching the flower parts between layers of sticky paper helps prevent the plant parts from losing their shape.

More Fun Things to Know and Do

Plant parts can be used to create your own design. A flower design can be made as follows:

- Repeat steps 1 to 6 of the original experiment.

- Use the marker to draw a face on the sticky surface of the Contact paper.

- Place the flower petals and leaves around the face, as shown.

- ADULT STEP Remove the backing from the second piece of Contact paper and place it over the flowers and frame.

- Repeat steps 9 to 13 to finish your picture.

Appendix
Section Summaries

Basic Life-Forms

Animals, like all living things, are made of building blocks called **cells**. Most cells are very small and flexible. But bone cells have calcium substances between them that give bones their hardness. Some animal cells are so small that a line of 40,000 of these cells would be about 1 inch (2.5 cm) long. In the experiment "Building Blocks" (pages 6–9), children make two models, an animal cell and an animal. The cell model contains these parts: the **cell membrane** (the lining around the cell which holds the cell together), the **cytoplasm** (the jellylike fluid that the cell parts float in), the **nucleus** (the control center of the cell which directs all the cell's activities), and the **mitochondria** (the power stations of the cell where food and oxygen react to produce the energy needed for the cell to work and live).

The four parts of the cell model made in "Building Blocks" are common to both animals and plants. Two cell parts found only in plant cells are **chloroplasts** (green bodies in which food for the plant is made) and a **cell wall** (a stiff wall-like structure on the outside of the cell membrane). In the experiment "Stiff" (pages 10–13), a basic model of a plant cell is made to show that it isn't bones that give plants their structure but the stiff cell wall. How water contributes to the firmness of a plant's structure is also shown.

Natural sources of water, such as ponds, lakes, and streams, usually contain single-celled organisms, even if the water looks crystal clear. In the experiment "Water Critters" (pages 14–17), children make models that demonstrate the movements of two types of single-celled microscopic water organisms: a paramecium and a euglena. The **paramecium**, or "slipper animal," found in and around the scum of quiet ponds, moves by fluttering the tiny hairs, called **cilia,** that cover the outside of its body. The **euglena**, found in fresh-water ponds and streams, moves by whipping a long, hairlike structure called a **flagella**. The euglena is interesting because it has both animal and plant parts.

Predators and Prey

A **predator** is an animal that hunts and eats other animals. The animal that becomes the meal for the predator is called the **prey**. Because of **camouflage** (colors and/or patterns on an animal's body that help the animal blend in with its environment), some animals avoid becoming a meal. **Chameleons** are lizards whose skin can change color. The color changes are usually from green to yellow or brown. These changes are a result of changes in temperature, light, and even the lizard's moods. Often the changes make the animal blend in with its environment, but not always. The experiment "Blending" (pages 20–23) demonstrates how colors can protect an animal from its predators.

Many animals, such as cats, are **nocturnal** (active at night). Cats need to be able to see well in order to hunt small animals in the dark, so their eyes have special features. The experiment "Bright Eyes" (pages 24–27) demonstrates two of these features. First, the shiny reflective layer at the back of the eye, called the **tapetum**, reflects light and causes the eye to glow. This increases the chances that the light will come in contact with the light-sensitive cells inside the cat's eye. Second, the **pupil** (the black opening in the center of the eye) **dilates** (enlarges) in the dark to let in more light.

Some birds, such as whippoorwills and sparrows, have large, gaping mouths that act like nets to capture insects in the air. These birds have facial bristles near the mouth that increase their ability to catch flying prey. Woodpeckers have hard bills and swordlike tongues that enable them to dig out and spear insects in wood. The experiment "Catchers" (pages 28–31) demonstrates how large-mouthed birds catch flying insects and how woodpeckers dig insects out of trees.

A spiderweb is made of **silk** (a fine, soft fiber produced by certain insects and spiders). The silk is a liquid protein produced by silk glands, called **spinnerets**, within the spider's abdomen. The liquid silk solidifies as it comes in contact with the air. Spiders produce different kinds of silk; some is sticky and some is not. Some spiders stand in the hub of their web with their eight legs on the nonsticky support strands that lead out from the hub. Insects that fly into the sticky snare get stuck. When the spider feels the strands move as the insect wriggles in an effort to escape, it quickly moves toward the trapped insect. The spider usually kills the insect with a poisonous bite and may wrap it in silk threads for a later meal. The experiment "Snare" (pages 32–35) demonstrates the differences in the strands a spider uses to spin a web and explains why the spider does not get caught in the web. Children also learn how to collect spiderwebs.

Body Temperature

Some animals, such as dogs, are not able to sweat to cool off, so instead they pant. When a dog pants, water from its tongue **evaporates** (changes from a liquid to a gas). In the process, the water takes heat energy away from the skin, causing the skin to cool. The experiment "Chill Out" (pages 38–41) demonstrates the cooling effect of evaporation.

The fur and feathers of animals **insulate** (reduce the escape of heat) their bodies. Some animals that live in very cold environments also have a thick layer of **blubber** (insulating fat) under their skin. The experiment "Overcoats" (pages 42–44) demonstrates the insulating ability of fur or feathers and blubber.

Animal Movement

Even though some squirrels are called flying squirrels, they cannot fly. These squirrels have special flaps of skin stretched between their front and hind legs. When the squirrel leaps from one branch to another, the skin is stretched out like sails to help it glide. The experiment "Glider" (pages 46–49) demonstrates how flying squirrels glide.

A two-legged animal, such as a bird, a human, or an ape, stays balanced as long as its **center of gravity** (the point at which an object balances) does not extend past its foundation (the feet). When an animal raises its leg to walk, its body leans slightly to the side opposite the raised leg to redistribute the body's weight and again place its center of gravity over the supporting leg. The experiment "Balanced" (pages 50–53) demonstrates how leaning helps two- and four-legged animals maintain balance when walking.

Liquids, such as water, push up on objects in it. This upward force is called **buoyancy**. If the weight of the object is spread out, the water under the object can lift it to the surface and hold it there. Thus, the object floats. A fish rises or sinks by taking in or releasing air from a balloonlike organ called a **swim bladder**. This air changes the weight of the fish, but it is the change in size that affects it most. As the amount of air inside the fish's bladder increases, the fish enlarges. Since it takes up more space in the water, there is more water pushing up on it. Thus, it rises. The experiment "Floaters" (pages 54–57) demonstrates how fish rise and sink in water.

An octopus moves along the sea bottom using its eight long arms. Like other sea organisms, such as squid and jellyfish, it can jet propel itself through the water by expelling water. **Jet propulsion** is the forward movement of a body that results as a reaction to the rearward discharge of a forceful stream of fluid. The experiment "Squirters" (pages 58–61) demonstrates the movement of octopi and jellyfish. Children also make a model that explains the physical features of a jellyfish.

Plant Growth

The outer protective covering of a seed is called the **seed coat**. This covering helps protect the inside of the seed from insects, disease, and damage. **Beans** are a smooth, hard seed that is eaten as a vegetable. The two parts of the bean that are pried apart, called **cotyledons** or **seed leaves**, contain the first food for the growing embryo. Plants with two seed leaves, such as beans, are called **dicotyledons** or **dicots**. Those with one seed leaf, such as corn, are called **monocotyledons** or **monocots**. The tiny plantlike structure inside the bean looks like a baby plant, but it is correctly called an **embryo**

(the part that develops into a plant). In the experiment "Baby Plants" (pages 64–67), children take apart seeds of various dicots to reveal the embryo inside each.

Germination is the plant process of developing from a seed into a plant. Seeds can germinate and grow almost anywhere if they have the right temperature, water, and air. The experiment "Anywhere?" (pages 68–71) demonstrates that seeds do not need soil or light to germinate; however, minerals from the soil and light are necessary for plants to be healthy and to develop properly. (See the experiment "Thirsty Plant," pages 82–85, for information about how plants get minerals from the soil.)

A **seed** is the part of a plant formed in the flower. It contains the embryo and stored food.

Beans and other seeds from around the kitchen will grow if they have not been cooked or otherwise injured. The heat of cooking will kill the embryo inside the seed. In the experiment "Sprouters" (pages 72–75), children plant beans and other seeds to see whether they will grow.

Growth of a plant toward light is called **phototropism**. *Photo* means light and *tropism* means turning. This type of growth occurs when plant chemicals cause cells on the dark side of the plant stem to grow longer than those on the light side. Longer cell growth on one side of the stem causes the stem to curve. Thus, the stem curves or turns toward the light. In the experiment "Sun Seekers" (pages 76–79), plants are observed to grow toward sunlight.

Plant Parts

Sap is the watery liquid in plants. Sap moving from the roots contains water with minerals from the soil dissolved in it. Sap moves from the roots of plants through **xylem tubes** (tiny transport tubes in plants) to the leaves and other plant parts, depositing minerals throughout the plant. Some of the water is used by the plant and some evaporates through **stomata** (tiny holes in the leaves). The loss of **water vapor** (water in the gas state) into the atmosphere through the stomata of plants is called **transpiration**. As water transpires from the leaves, more water and minerals are pulled in at the roots. The experiment "Thirsty Plant" (pages 82–85) lets children see how water moves through plants.

Cacti and other desert plants store water. Some cacti, such as the saguaro, have a pleated surface that allows them to expand with water during wet periods. These cacti may increase in size as much as 20 percent during the rainy season. During times of no rain, they use up their stored water and shrink back to a smaller size and shape. Desert plants have other ways of reducing the amount of water vapor lost through transpiration. Having thick, wavy, coated leaves and stems is one way of doing this. The experiment "Juicy" (pages 86–89) demonstrates how cacti and other desert plants store and retain water.

White light, including sunlight, is made up of all the colors in the rainbow. You see objects as having different colors because of **pigments** (chemicals that give color to materials) in them that reflect different colors of light to your eyes. The green pigment in plants is called **chlorophyll.** In the experiment "Plant Paints" (pages 90–93), children use plant pigments as paint.

The flesh of bananas and other fruits, such as pears and apples, discolors when the fruit is peeled and the flesh is exposed to air. This discoloration happens when oxygen in the air combines with the fruit. Vitamin C, which occurs naturally in lemons and other citrus fruits, combines with the oxygen before the oxygen gets to the fruit. The experiment "Browning" (pages 94–97) shows how vitamin C can be used to prevent the darkening of peeled bananas.

Flowers

Honey guides are markings on flower petals that lead bees to the center of the flower, where the **nectar** (a sugary liquid produced by flowers) is stored. Not all honey guides are visible to the human eye but they can all be seen by the eyes of a bee. Most flowers have the same general structure. The **pistil** is the female reproductive organ that contains **eggs** (female reproductive cells) and is where seeds are formed. It is in the center of the flower surrounded by **stamens** (male reproductive organs where pollen is formed). **Pollen** is the yellow dustlike powder that contains **sperm** (male reproductive cells). The combination of an egg and sperm results in the formation of a seed. The **petals** and **sepals** are leaflike structures that surround and protect the flower's reproductive organs. The sepals surround the petals. When a bee enters a flower to drink the nectar, some of the pollen sticks to the legs and other hairy parts of its body. As the bee flies from flower to flower, pollen drops off and some lands on top of the pistils, which are sticky. When flowers are **pollinated** (pollen is transferred from stamen to pistil), a seed is formed in the pistil. In the experiment "Guides" (pages 100–103), children make a model of a flower showing honey guides. They also make a model of a bee that collects "pollen" on its feet and legs from the flower model.

Morning glories open every morning because sap moves through the xylem tubes into the cells of the closed petals, pushing the petals open. Some flowers open more quickly than others, but most open too slowly to be seen. When leaves of sensitive plants, such as mimosa and Venus's-flytrap, are touched, they can close within seconds. The experiment "Morning Glories" (pages 104–107) demonstrates in an exaggerated way the movement of sap into closed flowers.

The oil in many sweet-smelling flowers serves multiple purposes. It is used in making perfume, and it also attracts pollinators, such as insects, to the flowers. Not all flowers have sweet-smelling oils. The rafflesia, a Malaysian plant, smells like rotting meat. The flowers of this plant are pollinated by flies attracted to the stinky smell. In the experiment "Scented" (pages 108–111), children make perfume from the sweet-smelling oil in the petals of garden flowers. They also learn which kinds of insects are attracted to these flowers.

Plants can be temporarily preserved by arranging them between sheets of Contact paper. This method flattens and holds the plant parts as they **dehydrate** (lose water). In the experiment "Keepers" (pages 112–115), children learn this method of preserving plants.

Glossary

bean A smooth, hard seed that is eaten as a vegetable.

blubber A thick layer of insulating fat under the skin of some animals that live in cold environments, such as seals, whales, and walruses.

buoyancy The upward force that a liquid, such as water, exerts on objects floating in it.

camouflage Colors and/or patterns on an animal's body that help the animal blend in with its environment.

cell A building block of living things.

cell membrane The lining around a cell which holds the cell together.

cell wall The stiff wall-like structure on the outside of the cell membrane of plants.

center of gravity The point at which an object balances.

chameleon A lizard with skin that can change from green to yellow or brown.

chlorophyll The green pigment in plants.

chloroplasts Green bodies in a plant cell that contain chlorophyll and in which food for the plant is made.

cilia Tiny hairlike structures around the outside of some one-celled organisms, such as the paramecium, that are used for movement.

cotyledon The part of a seed that contains the first food for the plant embryo; also called **seed leaf**. See also **dicotyledon** and **monocotyledon**.

cytoplasm The jellylike fluid that the parts of a cell float in.

dehydrate To lose water or to remove water from.

dicotyledon or dicot A plant that has two seed leaves.

dilate To enlarge.

egg Female reproductive cell.

embryo (plant) The tiny plantlike structure inside a seed from which a plant develops.

euglena Microscopic organism found in freshwater ponds and streams.

evaporate To change from a liquid to a gas due to absorption of energy, such as heat.

flagella A long hairlike structure on some one-celled organisms, such as the euglena, that is used for movement.

germination The plant process of developing from a seed into a plant.

honey guides Markings on flower petals that lead bees to the center of the flower, where the nectar is stored.

insulate To reduce the escape of energy, such as heat, from an object.

jet propulsion The forward movement of a body that results as a reaction to a rearward discharge of a forceful stream of fluid.

mitochondria (singular **mitochondrion**) The power stations of a cell where food and oxygen react to produce the energy needed for the cell to work and live.

monocotyledon or monocot A plant that has one seed leaf.

nectar A sugary liquid produced by flowers.

nocturnal Active at night.

nucleus The control center of a cell which directs all the cell's activities.

paramecium ("slipper animal") Microscopic organism found in and around the scum of quiet ponds.

petals Leaflike structures that surround and protect a flower's reproductive organs.

phototropism The growth of a plant toward light.

pigments Chemicals that give color to materials.

pistil The female reproductive organ in the center of a flower where seeds are formed.

pollen The yellow dustlike powder produced by the stamens that contains sperm.

pollination The transfer of pollen from stamen to pistil.

predator An animal that hunts and eats other animals.

prey An animal that becomes a meal for a predator.

pupil The black opening in the center of the eye.

sap Watery liquid in plants.

seed A plant part formed in the flower and containing the embryo and stored food.

seed coat The outer protective covering of a seed.

seed leaf See **cotyledon**.

sepals Leaflike structures around a flower's petals that, with the petals, help to protect the flower's reproductive organs.

silk A fine, soft fiber that is a liquid protein produced by spinnerets within the abdomen of certain insects and spiders and that is used by spiders to make webs.

sperm Male reproductive cell.

spinnerets Silk-making glands in the abdomen of certain insects and spiders.

stamen The male reproductive organ of a flower, where pollen is formed.

stomata (singular **stoma**) Tiny holes in the leaves of plants.

swim bladder A balloonlike organ that helps a fish rise or sink by taking air in or releasing it from the organ.

tapetum The shiny reflective layer at the back of the eye of some animals, such as cats.

transpiration The loss of water vapor into the atmosphere through the stomata of plants.

water vapor Water in the gas state.

xylem tubes Tiny transport tubes in plants that carry sap from the roots to the leaves and other plant parts.

Index